Far From The Tree

Poetic Musings Across Three Generations

PHILLIP EUGENE WILLIAMS

PHYLLIS WILLIAMS-STRAWDER

MORGAN P. STRAWDER

ESPRESSO MISCHIEF
Strong - Bold - Intentional

Far From The Tree
Phyllis Williams-Strawder
espressomischief@gmail.com

Published 2019, by Espresso Mischief Publishing
www.espressomischief.com
hello@espressomischief.com
(562) 356-8111
Medford, OR 97501 USA

Paperback ISBN: 978-1-7330957-4-7
Ebook ISBN: 978-1-7330957-5-4
Library of Congress Control Number 2019909747

Printed and Bound in the United States Of America
First Printing August 2019

DEDICATION

This book is dedicated in memory of my father,
Phillip e,
the original poet.

It's also dedicated to all the fragile, strong, right, and wrong family
relationships in the world.

Works By
Phyllis Williams-Strawder

That Damn Girl Stuff: A Mother's Truth

Finding Life Balance

Editor

The Secret To Her Heart, 2nd Edition
The Dating Man's Cookbook

Spice: The Variety Of Life

Works By
Morgan P. Strawder

little girl BIG JOB

Morgan Mischief:@ the end of the day
(co-authored with Phyllis Williams-Strawder)

Let's Be Social
@SpressoMischief
@MorganMischief

Walk with Love

Speak with Love

Touch with Love

Listen with Love

Whatever it is you do, do it with Love

LOVE IS EVERYTHING

Train up a child in the way he should go and when he is old, he will not depart from it. -
Prov 22:6 KJV

Far From The Tree

Poetic Musings Across Three Generations

How far we've come
How far removed
From roots that run so deep

You sow a seed
You work the field
You water as you weep

The sun beams down
The day awaits
On a harvest yet to reap

How far we've come
How far removed
From roots that run so deep

HEALTH

Health! What is it?

Is it yours or mine? Take it or leave it.
Bad or good? I hope it's good.
May I take it?

The good one?

Nothing bad.
No shots.
No cherry barf medicine.
No thermometers.
None of that.

Perfect condition.

I'll use it for fun.
I'll look in mom and dad's ears
And eyes, nose, ugh, boogies.
Only for fun.
I'll give some to mom and dad.

Good health!

Don't want them sick.
No hospitals.
Give it to everyone.

Good health!

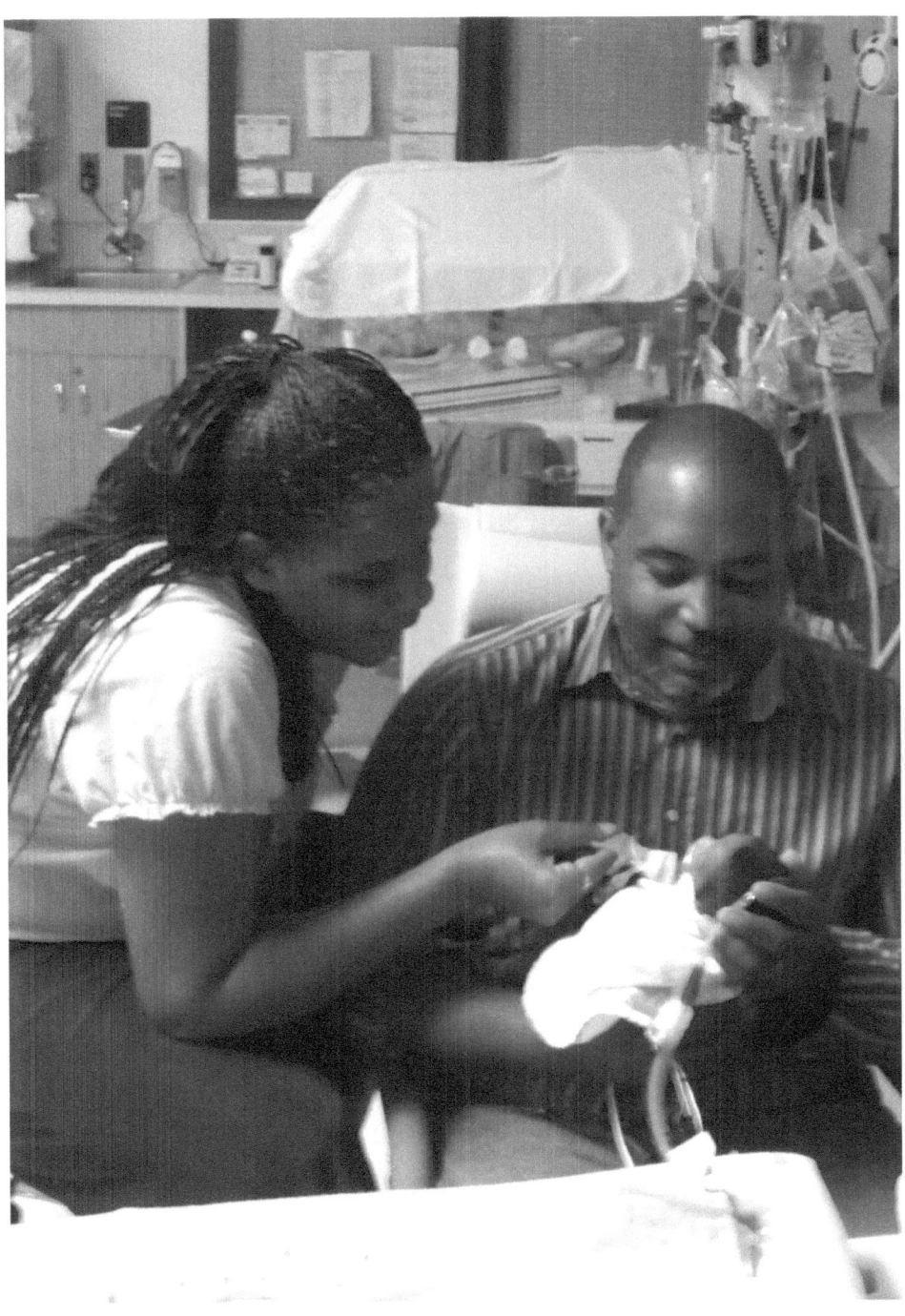

Birthing A Blessing

Twice I tried and both they died
I prayed for you and yet I cried
What if you didn't make it through
What if God requested you

If God proclaimed you were just for me
I just had to wait and see
But as I stood I wet the floor
Three more months was out the door

You entered the world without a sound
My heart was full and thoughts abound
I refused to worry, I refused to fret
Cause in God's hand there is no threat

My tears were free in my solemn cry
I prayed Dear Lord don't let her die
He heard my prayers through faith so worn
He blessed my life when you were born

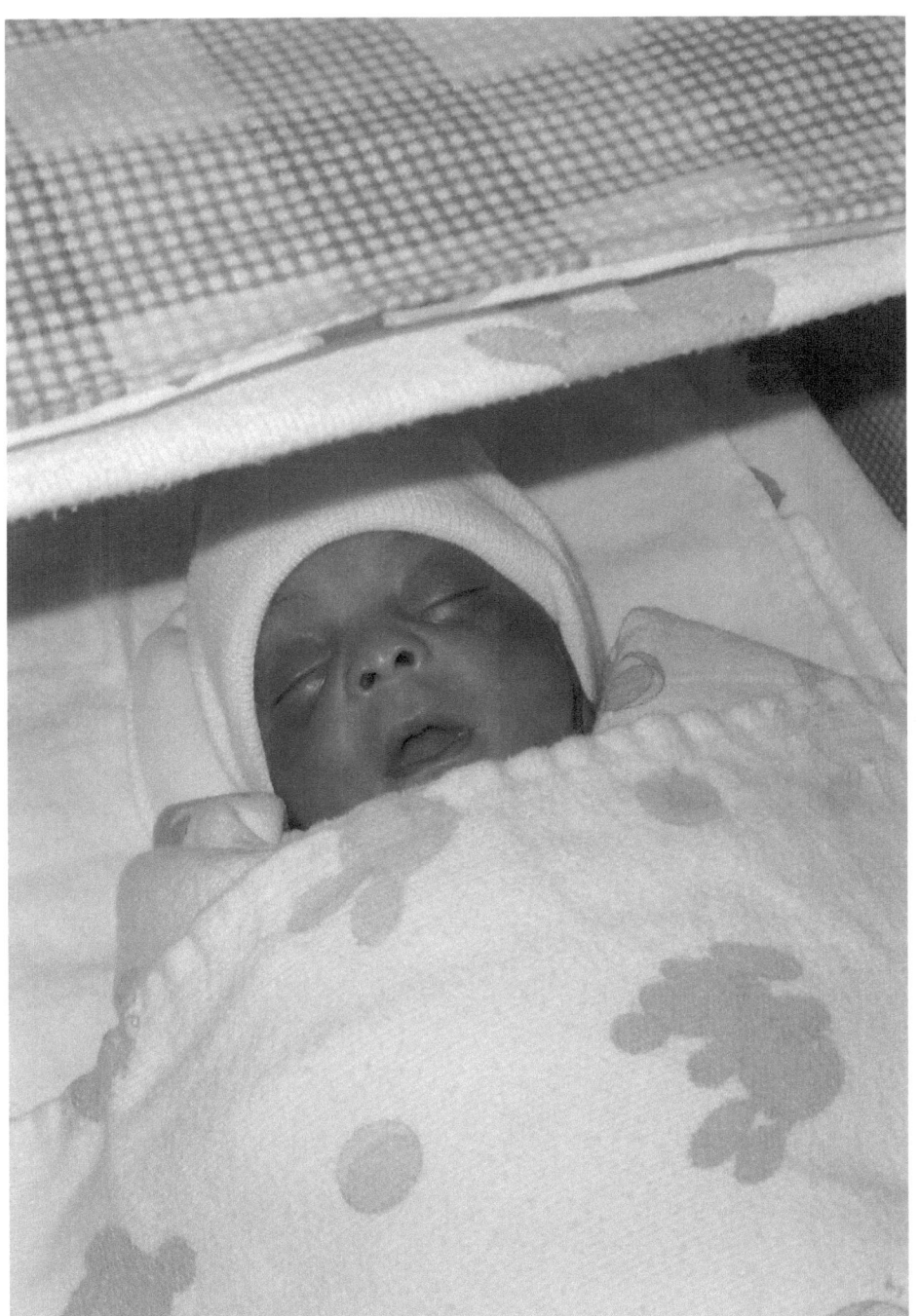

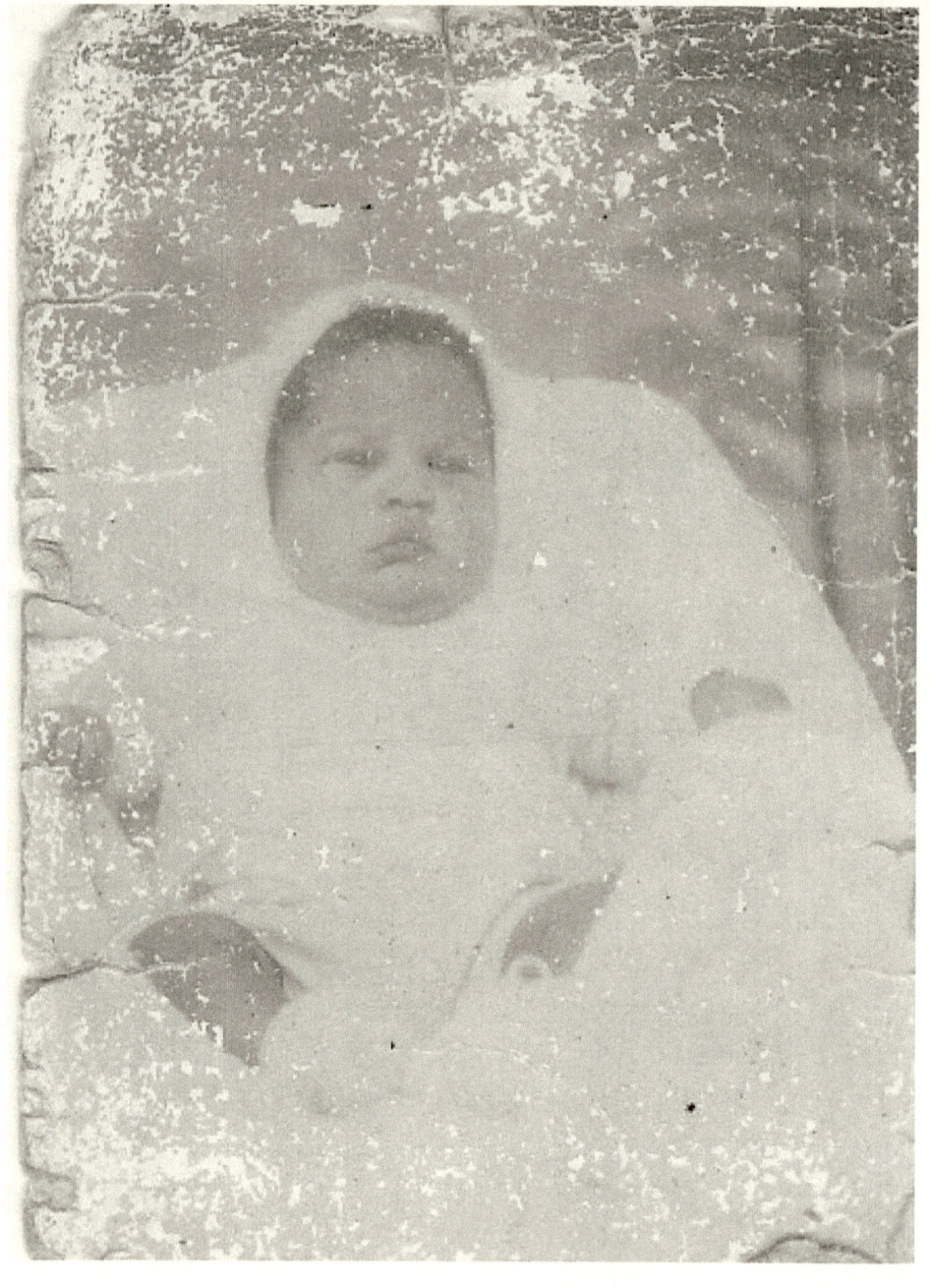

Arise and Live

When the Sun rises to awaken you from your slumber,
To the opportunity to live the dream of a conscience life;
May the choices of your actions bloom with beauty,
Never before seen and without strife;

As your day's labor prepares you for your tomorrow,
You should find pleasure, in the sweat of your brow;
Understand... it was your day to produce,
Even though you knew not how;

Know the fruit is sweet and tasty,
As you ingest the flavors of God's love;
As the moon announces... Another day is done,
Give thanks to Him... Who has sent it from above.

Philip e

CANDY WRAPPER ME

Tossed aside once the good part is out,

Left on the sidewalk to be blown about,

That's me, you see,

As worn as can be.

Do not fret for me!

Perhaps I'll contribute to pollute the sea.

You could pick me up!

You could blow me down!

Make me into something else,

How does that sound?

OH DEAR!

A strong gust of wind,

Blows me left,

Right through your fingers!

And no matter how hard you try,

To lift me up,

I'll be gone,

To perhaps distract a pup.

Hard Candy You

Her view of the world still young and new

The gust she feels are innocent too

I raise her to be true and strong

But still she's sweet don't get it wrong

My mouth speaks lessons I hope she hears

But I know some things will cause her tears

They grind her down, I lift her high

I constantly say reach for the sky

A mother has the right to dream big dreams

But inside is a mother's constant screams

Don't do this and don't touch that

Leave him alone, he wants your cat

Some lessons she'll learn all on her own

But I have faith good seeds I've sown.

Morgan P:

Words can not express the pounding in my Chest,
That occurred when I saw your Smile;
But I am assured you will pass every Test,
To become your Grand Folk's very best Grandchild.
I love you mightily with all my heart,
Watching you grow makes me just say wow!
So do what you do and know I love you,
You're qualified to take a second bow.
Your Grand Dad

Phillip e

NUM NOMS

Today we will talk about food.

But not the kind that fills your belly.

The hunger of passion,

Not of pain,

Of joy.

The fire in your eyes

That fills them with determination.

What do you want to eat?

I want to fill with the hunger for joy,

By fulfilling my passion.

More Than What She Seems

You see a girl.

I see the hopes and dreams of generations past

You see a girl

I see my future in ways that will last

You see girl

I see my mom whose eyes filled with joy

You see a girl

I see her father whose worried bout boys

You see a girl

I see a young lady who's confident and smart

You see a girl

I see the boy who may break her heart.

You see a girl

I see a woman who knows her self-worth

You see a girl

I see my future to whom I've given birth

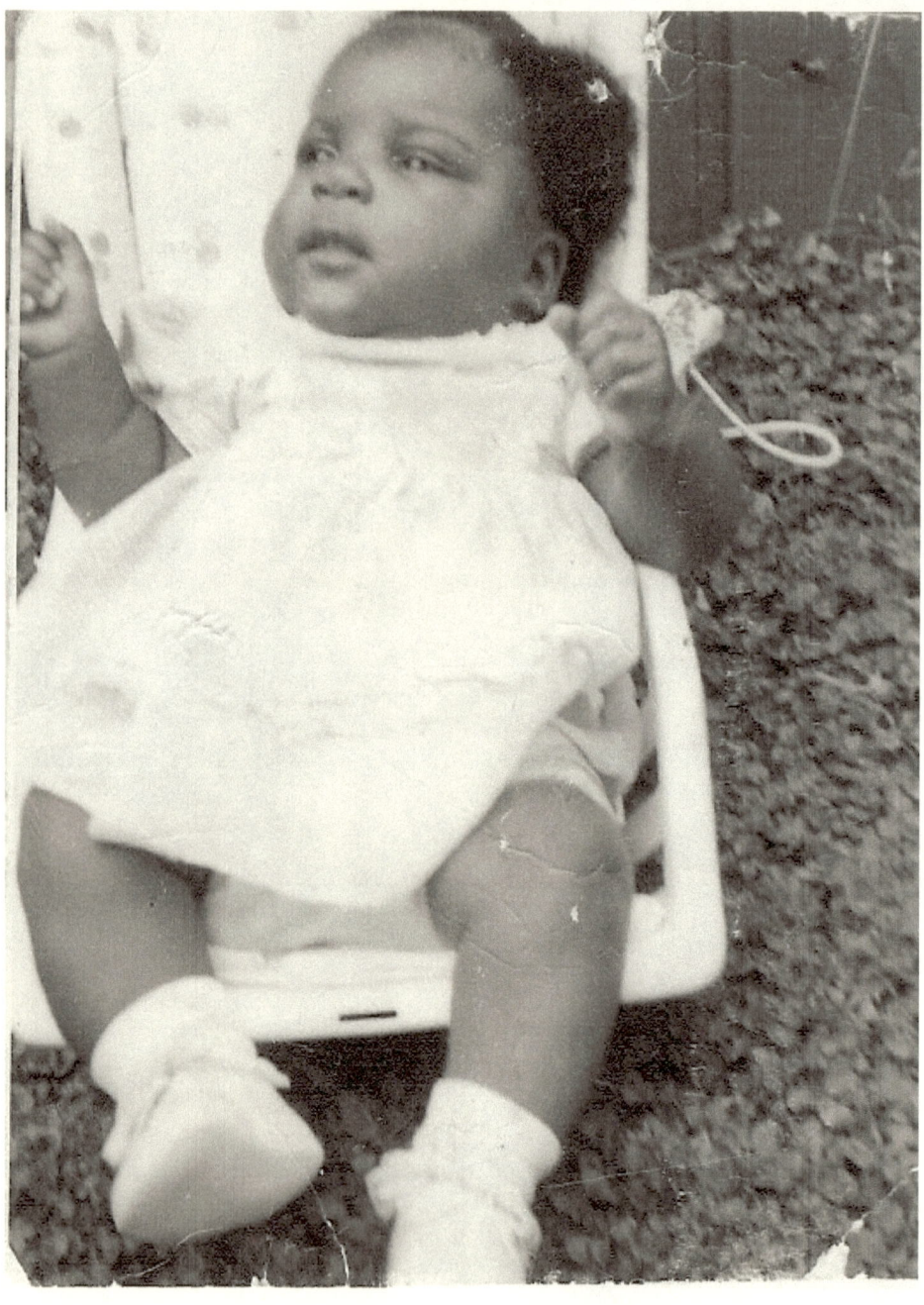

What do you see?

Do you see what I see, when I look at me
Or do you see, what you think me to be;
What reflection of God perfection is distorted by the
thoughts of man?
What beauty is found in the castle made of sand?
It is what it is, no matter what sight you behold
We must know it's from our minds, all things unfold;
From the spiritual realm, all things come
Available to all, for we are one;
Now look again at me, what do you see;
I am your perception of what God made me to be.

Phillip e

MOUNTAINS

Right now they are little hills,

Quite perky and small,

But one day, they'll be as big as my mother's!

Sagging with gravity and all…

You know what never mind,

That's not what I want.

Mine will be better

Then her I will taunt!

Yet and still, at the end of the day,

Mine are still perky and small.

The day is coming when my little hills

Will not be little hills at all

Mountains Out Of Mole Hills

If you were older I'd say some things

If I said them now the words would sting

Your breast are pert and mine may sag

Yours may jiggle while mine may wag

But go ahead and have your laugh

Just remember you're my genetic half

Cause gravity is not your true friend

And your day will come when yours descend

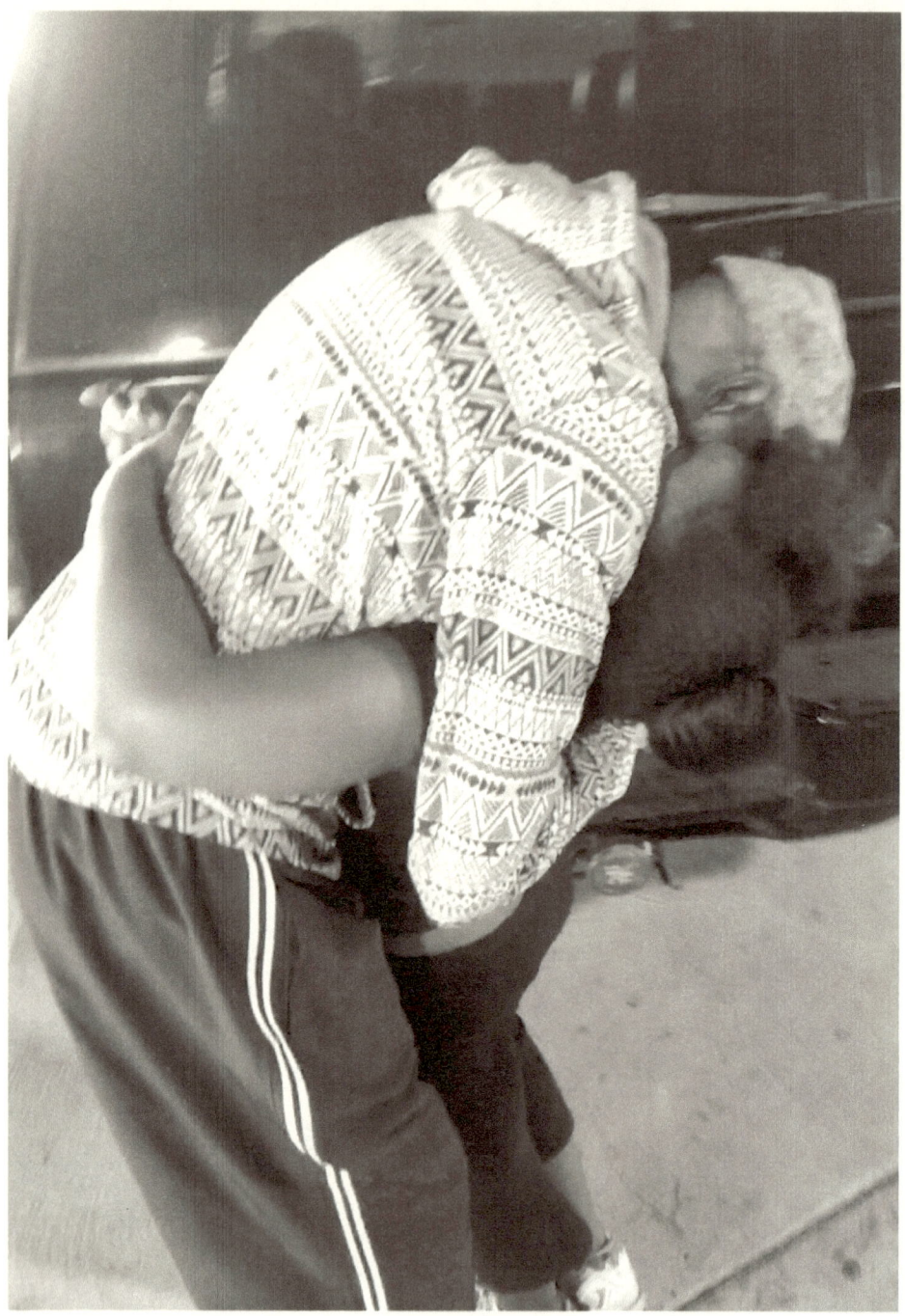

May the seeds of your Dreams,
Be the Harvest of your Future;
May the Angel of Prosperity,
Be Allowed To Guide your Steps;
May God's Loving Grace,
Forever Bless Your Desire.

Phillip e

MONKEYS CAN'T FLY

Monkeys can climb.

Eagles can fly.

Fish can swim.

Cats can jump.

Dogs can bark.

People can die.

                                    And that's about it

One thing they can do,

Is live their life.

But those who don't live die.

                                    And that's about it

Who You're Meant To Be

You try so hard to be something you're not

It's futile and yet you persist

You go through the motions of not being you

Your own image you try to resist

There's nothing wrong with figuring things out

There are lots of things you can try

When all's said and done if you're not happy with you

Then you should stop living a lie

Your reality is a state of mind. Your state of mind determines your reality. Therefore your freedom and your environment determines the measure of your state of mind.

Phillip e

HAPPINESS

Happiness is something

    We can never obtain

        We want 'this' and 'that'

            We can never refrain

        We live with this thing called jealousy

    We want what others get you see

From the best slice of cake

    To the bestest new toy

        And for a short while

            We are filled with great joy

        But we all grow old, here only a while

    All of our toys left in a pile

        So you shouldn't be jealous

            Because you will leave too

                So why don't you live

                    Because days can seem few

Joy From Within

Joy found in people, place or things

Is fleeting to say the least

Joy from your soul and spirit

Is joy of a bountiful feast

While those around can make you smile

They can't give you lasting joy

It's when you can smile for no reason at all

That's a joy you should always employ

When you do little dances and people shoot glances

You'll wonder why they're so annoyed

Pay them no mind and shake your behind

You've learned how to live overjoyed

How do you forgive, when you can't forget?
You must bury the pain, before you go insane;
It is your choice to forgive, or continue to re-live;
But how?
You must focus on 'Now!
Because it is what it is,
'What' will be – will be;
That's what it is; what you can change you change;
What you can't, you won't,
That's life,-live it.

Phillip e

TRAVEL

Go where you want in the world.

To a tree or across the Americas.

Where would you like to go?

You choose.

I can't take you.

I can't make you.

I can't pay.

You choose.

With family or all alone.

Peace and quiet.

Loud and proud.

Surrounded by what you love.

You choose.

The World Awaits

There's nothing to fear if done the right way

So travel the world, find new places to stay

Good and bad things happen wherever you go

Don't allow fear to wreck how you flow

Open yourself to new things, new cultures, new ways

Stop living in fear as if you were prey

Good and bad people cover the world

Don't live as a flower never blooming or unfurled

By air, by train, however you stray

Get up and get out and travel your way

Tigers Set New Record

The Toul Tigers balanced their league record to 11 wins against 11 losses for the season when they ormped the SHAPE Indians both games of the series on 5-6 February.

On Saturday evening the TRAB netmen set a high scoring record for the base gymnasium swishing a grand total of 117 points while establishing a high score record in the France District League.

Opposing players move in as Tiger, Phil Williams, (#30) jumps for a rebound against SHAPE netman in the second half of play, Friday. Tigers defeated the SHAPE Indians both games of the series. (Photo by Simon)

What is Great

Well it is not; to late,
To determine what is great;
Who's to decide the serving on your plate,
What it is that will determine your fate;

It is the goals you must set for yourself,
Not the ones you've relegate to the shelf;
It's in the end when you've have passed the Pearly Gate,
That will determine that you've been determined Great!

Phillip e

CRANKY OL' LADY

I used to know a cranky ol' woman,
But boy did she love to laugh!
I used to know a frowny ol' woman,
But boy did she love to smile!
I used to know a scared ol' woman,
But boy was she brave and bold!
I used to know a fussy ol' woman,
But boy did she love to help!
I used to know a good ol' woman
I loved her smile, her laugh, everything about her.
She was my grandmother
All cranky.
But not in the least bit.
That's why I loved her.
Everything she seemed
She was not.
She's gone.
I miss her.
But she's here.
Watching from heaven in my heart

Don'Talk About My Momma

How dare she talk about my momma like that,
I'm the only one allowed to call her cranky like that.
That cranky ol' laugh, with her cranky ol' ways,
How dare you say that since she's used up her days.

That frowny ol' lady had earned every crease,
In my early days I didn't give her much peace.
That scared ol' lady had been through a lot,
That's why towards the end brave and bold you got.

That fussy ol' lady tried to keep me in line,
But when it came to you, her bark was benign.
That good ol' lady gave her time and her heart,
Where you resided was the biggest part.

I miss her too and you're right she's still here.
I feel her presence whenever you're near.

Corn Or Stones

Prayers of faith or skepticism with hate;
Love and understanding or waiting while demanding;

Strong black woman what 's your image of a Black Man?
What's your choice... of how you want him to stand?

Are you standing by his side or using your power to divide?
Can you see that "ME" must become "WE", if together we are
to "BE"?

What excuses do you make not to give, but to take?
While our kids have to suffer, if we don't show love to one
another.

What are you gonna do, to help us pull through?
Will you give me a hand, so together we can stand?

Will it be corn to be used for seeds to grow...? or,
Will you throw stones at me... instead of Jim Crow?

Phillip e

RED!

Seeping through the fabric
Going unnoticed until day's end

Red
Staining my towel
Coloring my sheets

Red
Complicated shopping.
Reviews and references
Complicated uses.
Changing my preferences.

Red
I understand now, but why do I,
Or any girl for that matter,
Have to have a period? Le sigh

The Whiteness

No more worries
No more stains
No more bloating
No more pain

My clothes are drenched
Good Lord it's hot
Can't sleep at night
But still it's not

That monthly visit
From dear aunt flow
But one more flash
And I'm gonna blow

MY SOULMATE

The corniest line I ever heard was you complete me
But you complete my strength & my soul
No truer words could ever be
Now our two halves make a whole

I once believed I was better alone
I needed no one by my side
Yet through you in me a seed has grown
And my loneliness has gone and died

I wouldn't trade a single tear
I wouldn't trade one pain
Each time I cried I shed the fear
That felt like heavy chain

If not for you there'd be no her
But that's not what makes me whole
It's because you reached into my heart
And touched my very soul

Sister meets Mister

I keep smelling the aroma you left behind,
That's why I left my clothes on for a long, long time;
As thoughts of you dashed through my head,
As I wonder what you're like, the thought swiftly fled;
Remembering, in your arms is that sense of oneness,
Being engulfed with ecstasy, of immeasurable serenity.
Now I await the time to come, when again we're one,
Alone – "to be free and willing to be," what we begun.

Phillip e

TO MORGAN

When my life is done I hope you see
I want you to be the best you you can be
Take all my good and leave all my bad
Be better than me I won't be mad
Don't mourn my loss you have a life to live
And know any wrongs go to God to forgive
If the Lord allows I'll watch as you grow
You're my greatest joy forever and so

I leave with you blessings and love evermore
Be a blessing to others you'll be blessed even
more.